UNITED ANGEL AIRLINES

flight – 128

BOOKS 1 AND 2

CHRISTIAN AUTHOR

Bishop Royalty Jones

ISBN 978-1-950818-78-5 (paperback)

Copyright © 2020 by BISHOP ROYALTY JONES

All rights reserved. No part of this publication may be reproduced, distributed, or transmitted in any form or by any means, including photocopying, recording, or other electronic or mechanical methods without the prior written permission of the publisher. For permission requests, solicit the publisher via the address below.

Rev. date: 09/17/2020

Rushmore Press LLC
1 888 733 9607
www.rushmorepress.com

Printed in the United States of America

ALL PRAISES AND GLORY TO THE HOLY TRINITY-GOD THE FATHER-GOD THE SON JESUS-GOD THE HOLY SPIRIT

I WOULD LOVE TO THANK THE HOLY TRINITY-GOD THE FATHER- GOD THE SON-GOD THE HOLY SPIRIT FOR GIVING ME THE GIFT TO WRITE, A SOUND MIND TO CREATE A LOVE STORY THAT GIVES ALL THE HOPE AND THE BELIEF THAT YOU CAN HAVE ANYTHING YOUR HEART DESIRES. IF YOU DO NOT HAVE PARENTS OR PEOPLE THAT YOU FEEL THAT LOVE YOU GOD LOVES YOU AND WANTS FOR YOU TO HAVE THE BEST THAT LIFE HAS TO OFFER YOU. GOD WILL BRING PEOPLE IN YOUR LIFE THAT WILL HELP YOU IN SOME KIND OF WAY IF YOU JUST BELIEVE FOR YOURSELF THAT YOU CAN HAVE IT. GOD IS A GOD OF LOVE BUT FIRST YOU HAVE TO ALLOW YOURSELF TO HAVE LOVE IN A HEALTHY WAY TO GET HEALTHY LOVE BECAUSE EVERYONE THAT SAYS I LOVE YOU MAY NOT KNOW HOW TO LOVE IN A HEALTHY WAY. GOD'S LOVE IS ABOUNDING ACCORDING TO THE BIBLE IN WHICH I BELIEVE IN STATES IN JOHN 3:16 HOW GOD GAVE HIS SON FOR ALL OF US BECAUSE HE LOVES US BEYOND THE MIND OR HEART CAN IMAGINE.

I ALWAYS HAD THIS DREAM OF HAVING SOMEONE LOVE ME BEYOND MY HEART COULD MEASURE AND I DO IN THE HOLY TRINITY IN JESUS WHO TOOK THE TIME TO LEAVE ALL OF THE RICHES BEHIND FOR ALL OF US AND THEN TAKE ALL THE SINS WE HAD AND HAVE ON THE CROSS OF CALVARY SOMETHING THE DEVIL DO NOT WANT FOR YOU TO KNOW. I CANNOT EXPRESS HOW MUCH GOD LOVES US ALL BUT YET WE REALLY QUESTION ALL THE TIME DOES HE LOVE US. IF EVERYONE JUST READ THE BIBLE WITH YOUR HEART AND NOT YOUR MIND AS THOUGH IT IS A BOOK FOR THE CLASSROOM YOU WILL FIND THE STORY OF LOVE IN IT.

INTRODUCTION

THIS IS A LOVE STORY OF HOW GOD USES ANGELS TO CONNECT YOU TO A DESTINATION YOU NEVER SEEN COMING. THE ANGELS ALREADY KNOW YOUR DESTINATION AND WHO IS IN THE PLAN; HOWEVER, YOU HAVE NO CLUE OF WHAT GOD HAS PERFECTLY PLANNED FOR YOU OR YOUR FUTURE. AMANI WILLIAMS AND A HIGH RANKING OFFICER IS PUT TOGETHER WHEN HE DECIDES HE IS READY FOR HIS BRIDE. ALLEN OMMANJU- A HIGH RANKING OFFICER IN THE SERVICE PRAYS TO GOD FOR HIS BRIDE. HE LET GOD KNOW THAT HE IS READY FOR THE FOR FILLING PROMISE THAT HIS PEOPLE HAVE BEEN CHOSEN FOR, FOR MANY GENERATIONS TO COME. EVERY HIGH-RANKING OFFICER HAD THEIR TURN ON FLIGHT UNITED ANGEL AIRLINES- FLIGHT 128 TO FIND THEIR BRIDE. WHEN SOMEONE SAYS FLIGHT 128 THE ANGELS ARE IN POSITION TO GO FORTH WITH THE PLAN THAT GOD HAS IN STORE FOR THEM.

MATTHEW 20:16

SO THE LAST SHALL BE THE FIRST, AND THE FIRST LAST: FOR MANY ARE CALLED, BUT FEW ARE CHOSEN.

TABLE OF CONTENTS

BOOK 1

CHAPTER 1:   GROWING UP AS A CHRISTIAN 1
CHAPTER 2:   THE DESIRES OF THE HEART
             AS A YOUNG GIRL 4
CHAPTER 3:   RAISED TO FOLLOW GOD 6
CHAPTER 4:   THE FIRST TWO COMMANDMENTS
             GREAT COMMANDMENTS 10
CHAPTER 5:   THE MORAL LAWS OF GOD 18
CHAPTER 6:   MOMMA AND ME WITH FAITH 29
CHAPTER 7:   OUT IN THE WORLD 39

UNITED ANGEL AIRLINES
flight - 128

BOOK 1

Amani Williams

I am Amani Williams and I grew up as a Christian. My Mom and Dad believed strongly in GOD and the Holy Trinity.

My Mom and Dad always told me that GOD had great plans for me and that GOD tells them what to do when it's time for this time and that time for me to get ready for his plan.

Mom and Dad always told me that if I follow the Bible it will lead me into all truth.

BIBLE

B= BASIC

I= INSTRUCTIONS

B=BEFORE

L=LEAVING

E=EARTH

They told me that if I ever had a question ask GOD through prayer and that he would answer me. The only thing that confused me was in what way was he going to answer? Through a movie - newspaper article- through Mom and Dad- through a dream or just everyday life? Mom and Dad always said that you will know when it was him that is answering a prayer for me. They also told me that when I pray they have to be done in a positive manner for good to be done, to help and not hurt anyone.

Mom and Dad taught me to look at the world as a big place of possibility with the help of GOD. Mom and Dad prayed all the time. In the morning, over the phone, over food, throughout the day, at night before bed, and at church.

Mom and Dad taught me how to thank GOD in the name of Jesus for everything. They said no matter how it looks GOD always has a plan.

I saw how it worked for them in everything so I began to try it for myself starting out very young.

Mom and Dad I called them but to everyone else it was:

> Pastor John Williams and First Lady Joanna Williams of " New Day and New Covenant Church.

Chapter 2

THE DESIRES OF THE HEART AS A YOUNG GIRL

As a young girl Mom and Dad showed me how to Love everything along with how a young man is to Love me. I wanted a LOVE like Mom and Dad.

Mom and Dad loved each other through the good, the bad, and when the storms are raging as they say.

I always heard my Mom and Dad ask each other for forgiveness all the time. After they forgive each other then they would hug and kiss.

I wanted love like that.

Don't get me wrong I heard Mom fuss at Dad about being late for supper and that now his food was cold. Ha Ha Ha Ha, or that he missed a button on his shirt for rushing out the door, or forgetting his lunch.

They taught me that a man is supposed to open the door, pull out my chair, be polite to me, buy me nice things, do for me when I cannot do for myself such as if I had a cold or something.

Chapter 3

RAISED TO FOLLOW GOD

Mom and Dad always told me that GOD will order my steps. At first I used to say OK, but not really sure of what that really meant. As I began to go places I would ask GOD to order my steps. Sometimes I would wander off to maybe come to someone hurt or in need of prayer.

Dad, Mom and then myself may have been out somewhere then GOD calls my name and then gives me instructions of what to do or where to go. I then follow what GOD tells me to do. Mom and Dad realized that the more I heard GOD'S voice and followed his instructions, the more he used me.

GOD used me to pray- pray - pray. I never get tired of praying because I get excited on the results.

Whenever GOD tells me to do something I don't question it I just do it. Mom and Dad look on with amazement because they don't tell me everything they may know. When GOD tells them what to do it may have been from a prayer they prayed or for an answer from a prayed question they may need to know the answer to for GOD to give them.

One time at church Sister Martha Brooks was worried about her daughter because she was so very sick that she had to be admitted into the hospital. Mom and Dad had been praying for her and the family. GOD told me to tell Mom and Dad to take me to her. Mom and Dad did. The next day she came home well. They never told me that she was in the hospital, but GOD did.

There were many other instances GOD used me for one thing or another. I never gave it another thought because it was just expected for GOD to speak to me to do something. It was just normal. I just obeyed. Mom and Dad always told me that GOD was my Father first before he allowed them to be my parents on Earth. He wants us to listen to him when he speaks to us and then follow him.

EPHESIANS 6:1

CHILDREN, OBEY YOUR PARENTS IN THE LORD: FOR THIS IS RIGHT.

Chapter 4

THE FIRST TWO COMMANDMENTS GREAT COMMANDMENTS

NEW TESTAMENT

LUKE 10:26-27

HE SAID UNTO HIM, WHAT IS WRITTEN IN THE LAW? HOW READEST THOU?

AND HE ANSWERING SAID, THOU SHALT LOVE THE LORD THY GOD WITH ALL THY HEART, AND WITH ALL THY SOUL, AND WITH ALL THY STRENGTH, AND WITH ALL THY MIND; AND THY NEIGHBOR AS THYSELF.

OLD TESTAMENT

DEUTERONOMY 6:5

AND YOU SHALL LOVE THE LORD YOUR GOD WITH ALL THINE HEART, AND WITH ALL YOUR SOUL, AND WITH ALL YOUR MIGHT.

NEW TESTAMENT

MATTHEW 22:37

JESUS SAID UNTO HIM, THOU SHALT LOVE THE LORD THY GOD WITH ALL THY HEART, AND WITH ALL THY SOUL AND WITH ALL THY MIND.

NEW TESTAMENT

MATTHEW 22:38

THIS IS THE FIRST AND GREAT COMMANDMENTS

NEW TESTAMENT

MATTHEW 22:39

AND THE SECOND IS LIKE UNTO IT THOU SHALT LOVE THY NEIGHBOR AS THYSELF.

NEW TESTAMENT

MATTHEW 22:40

ON THESE TWO COMMANDMENTS HANG ALL THE LAW AND THE PROPHETS.

NEW TESTAMENT

MARK 12:29

AND JESUS ANSWERED HIM OF THE FIRST OF ALL COMMANDMENTS IS HEAR O ISRAEL; THE LORD OUR GOD IS ONE LORD:

NEW TESTAMENT

MARK 12:30

AND THOU SHALT LOVE THY LORD THY GOD WITH ALL THY HEART, AND WITH ALL THY SOUL, AND WITH ALL THY MIND, AND WITH ALL THY STRENGTH;

NEW TESTAMENT

MARK 12:31

AND THE SECOND IS LIKE, NAMELY THIS, THOU SHALT LOVE THY NEIGHBOR AS THYSELF. THERE IS NON OTHER THESE.

OLD TESTAMENT

LEVITICUS 19:18

THOU SHALT NOT AVENGE, NOR BEAR ANY GRUDGE AGAINST THE CHILDREN OF THY PEOPLE, BUT THOU SHALT LOVE THY NEIGHBOR AS THYSELF: I AM THE LORD

NEW TESTAMENT

JAMES 2:8

IF YE FULFIL THE ROYAL LAW ACCORDING TO THE SCRIPTURE, THOU SHALT LOVE THY NEIGHBOR AS THYSELF, YE DO WELL.

Mom and Dad taught me THE FIRST TWO GREAT COMMANDMENTS at a very young age. They said that GOD can use me to change the world with THE TWO GREAT COMMANDMENTS because love is catchy.

My Mom and Dad tells me that a smile can change a frown in which is a smile upside down. They have always told me that everyone is not the same or is raised the same so we have to help them. The love that GOD has for us and the love we should have for each other.

I have found that through GOD using my Mom and Dad and now me I have been seeing a change.

Good things have been happening good for me by continuing to listen to GOD and also my parents.

Chapter 5

THE MORAL LAWS OF GOD

THE OLD TESTAMENT

EXODUS 20: 1-17

EXODUS 20: 1

AND GOD SPAKE, ALL THESE WORDS, SAYING,

EXODUS 20: 2

WHICH HAVE BROUGHT THEE OUT OF THE LAND OF EGYPT, OUT OF THE HOUSE OF BONDAGE.

EXODUS 20:3

THOU SHALT HAVE NO OTHER GODS BEFORE ME.

EXODUS 20: 4

THOU SHALT NOT MAKE UNTO THEE ANY GRAVEN IMAGE, OR ANY LIKENESS OF ANYTHING THAT IS IN HEAVEN ABOVE, OR THAT IS IN THE EARTH BENEATH, OR THAT IS IN THE WATER UNDER THE EARTH:

EXODUS 20: 5

THOU SHALT NOT BOW DOWN THY-
SELF TO THEM, NOR SERVE THEM: FOR
I THE LORD THY GOD AM A JEALOUS
GOD, VISITING THE INIQUITY OF THE
FATHERS UPON THE CHILDREN UNTO
THE THIRD AND FOURTH GENERA-
TION OF THEM THAT HATE ME;

EXODUS 20: 6

AND SHEWING MERCY UNTO THOU-
SANDS OF THEM THAT LOVE ME, AND
KEEP MY COMMANDMENTS.

EXODUS 20: 7

THOU SHALT NOT TAKE THE NAME OF THE LORD THY GOD IN VAIN; FOR THE LORD WILL NOT HOLD HIM GUILTLESS THAT TAKETH HIS NAME IN VAIN.

EXODUS 20: 8

REMEMBER THE SABBATH DAY, TO KEEP IT HOLY.

EXODUS 20: 9

SIX DAYS SHALT THOU LABOUR, AND DO ALL THY WORK:

EXODUS 20: 10

BUT THE SEVENTH DAY IS THE SABBATH OF THE LORD YOUR GOD: IN IT YOU SHALL NOT DO ANY WORK, YOU, NOR YOUR SON, NOR YOUR DAUGHTER, YOUR MANSERVANT, NOR YOUR MAIDSERVANT, NOR YOUR CATTLE, NOR YOUR STRANGER THAT IS WITHIN YOUR GATES:

EXODUS 20: 11

FOR IN SIX DAYS THE LORD MADE HEAVEN AND EARTH, THE SEA, AND ALL THAT IN THEM IS, AND RESTED THE SEVENTH DAY: WHEREFORE THE LORD BLESSED THE SABBATH DAY, AND HALLOWED IT.

EXODUS 20: 12

HONOUR THY FATHER AND THY MOTHER: THAT THY DAYS MAY BE LONG UPON THE LAND WHICH THE LORD THY GOD GIVETH THEE.

EXODUS 20: 13

THOU SHALT NOT KILL.

EXODUS 20: 14

THOU SHALT NOT COMMIT ADULTERY.

EXODUS 20: 15

THOU SHALT NOT STEAL.

EXODUS 20: 16

THOU SHALT NOT BEAR FALSE WITNESS AGAINST THY NEIGHBOR.

EXODUS 20: 17

THOU SHALT NOT COVET THY NEIGHBOR'S HOUSE, THOU SHALT NOT COVET THY NEIGHBOR'S WIFE NOR HIS MANSERVANT, NOR HIS OX NOR HIS ASS, NOR ANYTHINGS THAT IS THY NEIGHBOR'S.

My Mom and Dad also taught me the moral laws of GOD in which I stick to because I don't want to ever displease GOD.

Mom and Dad says that everyone makes mistakes but it has to be corrected right away and then ask GOD to forgive you and then others.

One day when I was in school Bobby grabbed my pencil off of my desk without asking me because he broke his and he wanted another one to use. His desk was right next to mine. I immediately said to him " THOU SHALT NOT STEAL"! He didn't even know what that meant. He yelled I didn't steal it I wanted and needed it so I took it off of your desk. I saw that you had another one.

The teacher called both of us up to the front and then took us both in the hallway to find out what happened. She asked us both who wanted to go first. I said that he can. She let him speak then myself. When he found out that he stole the pencil because he didn't ask me for it, he said I am sorry. I stated that it is forgive me . He said forgive me please. I forgave him, then gave him a hug. We both went back to the classroom happy. We then finished our work.

After class the teacher Ms. Hoffmeyer kept us to finish our meeting to make sure we both were alright. We were that is when we became friends.

While waiting to get picked up by our parents I showed him the MORAL LAWS OF GOD. I explained them to him one by one the way Mom and Dad explained them to me.

After that Bobby wanted to know more and more about GOD. He wanted to know more about the bible. I saw a change in him. He treated people better and smiled more and more. He used to be to himself and didn't really pay anyone any attention, as though no one else was there.

Chapter 6

MOMMA AND ME WITH FAITH

NEW TESTAMENT

HEBREWS 11:1

NOW FAITH IS THE SUBSTANCE OF THINGS HOPED FOR, THE EVIDENCE OF THINGS NOT SEEN.

HEBREWS 11:6

BUT WITHOUT FAITH IT IS IMPOSSIBLE TO PLEASE HIM: FOR HE THAT COMETH TO GOD MUST BELIEVE THAT HE IS, AND THAT HE IS A REWARDER OF THEM THAT DILIGENTLY SEEK HIM.

There is a play at school and I found out they are in need of people for the play. The play was Esther. I thought to myself that I would make a good Esther. Dad wasn't the one to pick me up from school today it was Mom. I could not wait to tell her. Where is Dad I asked before telling her the news. She said that he is away at a Conference. Mom knew that there was something going on. She said, hey its me Mom tell me what is going on! I wanted to tell them both at the same time. Since Dad is not here I blurted it out to Mom in excitement that there is a play at school and that I thought that I would be very good at the lead role.

We began to pray and then believed that it would happen. I still didn't tell Mom the name of the play. I wanted it to be a surprise.

I had my mind set to speak with the teacher in charge, Mr. Nelson to see if at all possible I can audition as Esther.

Mr. Nelson was in the auditorium getting the scripts out and ready to hang up the roles needed for the play when I entered the auditorium.

Hello Mr. Nelson I said happily. Hello Amani. How can I help you? Just as I was about to ask Jada burst through the door and asked for the leading role- Esther. I stood there with my mouth opened so wide a bunch of flies could have flown in. Ha Ha Ha Ha- here comes FAITH.

Mr. Nelson said well Jada I was just speaking with Amani who was here first to speak with me about something. Nervously I began to speak, I said Mr. Nelson I believe that I would make a great Esther. If Jada wants the role you can give it to her.

As Mr. Nelson was making a decision I was praying and thinking about the scripture Hebrews 11: 6. I finished praying and then said Amen.

Mr. Nelson asked me before he made his decision What was I doing? I said praying. He said what? I said praying. He pulled me to the side and asked me a series of questions.

1. Do you always pray? I said YES about everything.

2. Who taught you how to pray? I said my parents.

3. Why do you want the role of Esther? I said because I know the story of Esther and I thought that I would make a great Esther.

4. Do you believe that you got the part? I said YES!

5. He asked why do you think that? I said the scripture of Hebrews 11:1 and I told him that without FAITH that it was impossible to please GOD.

Mr. Nelson asked for me to stay over to the side while he spoke with Jada. He asked her the same questions that he asked me. He wrote down the questions he asked us both down on a piece of paper along with the answers we gave. He told the both of us to meet him in the auditorium tomorrow at the same time because he wanted to be sure of his decision. He said that it was an important role.

Mom came to ask me what happened because I told her that I would see about it today. I told her that I don't have an answer as of yet. I did not tell her about Jada and what happened with her, but GOD did!

She asked who is Jada? I told her that she is a girl at school. Why? She began to ask questions about her and her family. I usually don't hang out with a lot of people, but I try to be nice and smile to everyone.

Mom said that we should have a girls day with her and her Mom. I said that I will ask her.

The next day we met in the auditorium but, Mr. Nelson was not there. Ms. Hoffmeyer came from the back to tell us that Mr. Nelson was not there and for us to forgive him for not being here. He will get back to us in 2 days.

WE BOTH RESPONDED WITH A SURPRISING LOUD QUESTION. IN 2 DAYS?

So we just went to the lounge area so we could talk. Can you believe what just happened? I know right! I asked Jada what Mom told me to ask her. She said that she can call me to tell me what her Mom said. I said good and gave her my cell phone number. I told her that I had to meet my Mom. We parted ways. As I was walking away I said OK LORD IS THIS A TEST OF MY FAITH? IF IT IS I BELIEVE YOU AND I HAVE FAITH DOWN PAT. THY WILL BE DONE AMEN.

As I was getting in the car I saw Jada across the way looking sad. Mom said so what happened? Mom already knew what happened because GOD told her, but she did not tell me. I can tell by the way she was acting. I told her that Mr. Nelson was not going to be there for 2 days. I should find out then when he gets back. Mom said ok. Amani did you ask Jada about girls day? Yes I asked and she said that she is going to call when she gets home.

Jada calls to say her Mom says YES. We set up a time after school to meet up. Mom met her Mom - Samantha Brooks and I introduced my Mom, they hugged and then they followed us.

I didn't know that Jada didn't have any friends so we became good friends. She said that she would always see me smiling and speaking to everyone. She said she thought I was a popular girl but she was confused because she didn't see me with no one but Bobby after school reading. I just giggled.

While her Mom and my Mom were getting acquainted, so were we. She asked what were me and Bobby reading? I said the BIBLE. She said the BIBLE! In total shock. I answered YES we study together. She asked if she could study with us because she said that they go to church once in a while. I answered you sure can and that we study every day. If she wanted to, she could as well.

After school we met up at the same place to study the BIBLE. Jada had a lot of questions. GOD gave me the answers.

The day came to meet with Mr. Nelson again in the auditorium. We came in and Mr. Nelson was waiting with an answer of whom he chose.

Mr. Nelson said before I give my answer, I want to tell you that I have been watching both of you in order to make my decision. We both looked at each other and laughed. We told him that we are friends and that whomever he picked we would help each other.

Mr. Nelson was glad to hear that news. He picked me to be ESTHER because of my humility. Jada said that I would make a great QUEEN. I just smiled and said thank you to both of you.

JADA YELLED HAIL TO THE QUEEN!!!!!!! WE ALL LAUGHED.

After the big hoopla of the play Esther more people began to speak more to me than me to them. I guess I became the popular girl that Jada thought I was. I stayed humble and spoke to everyone. I feel that as long as I stay humble through all the blessings that GOD has for me then I am grounded I thought to myself.

Today is a new day. Through FAITH I HAVE SUCCEEDED.

Chapter 7

OUT IN THE WORLD

The thought of going from High School to College was a little intimidating; however having my friends made the transition a little comforting. We all got accepted to THE BEGINNING WORD BIBLE COLLEGE.

TRANSITION - NEW BEGINNINGS

We all have been CELEBRATING OUR SUCCESS OF GRADUATION AND NOW COLLEGE TOGETHER AS FRIENDS THAT BECAME FAMILY.

The next day after the big CELEBRATION my Dad called a meeting to see what is next with us all and our plans for COLLEGE. My Dad started with me and Mom first, then Jada and her Mom, then Bobby and his parents. He wanted to meet at Fogo De Chao for dinner and to spend more time with Bobby's parents Cindy and Richard Branch because they are always traveling for business.

All of the parents decided that we should live in the dorm rooms at school that will allow us to be away from home to get the experience that we need to become independent that will force us to make choices for ourselves and together. I am not so sure of what to expect while being there, but one thing I know for sure is that we all have GOD and each other. Four years together will be good for me to have friends that are a part of my family close to me and to pray with me.

All four years we stayed close together. We prayed together, ate breakfast, lunch, dinner and also studied together. Yes we made friends but, all in all, we stayed together. We felt that making friends with others was good; however, our goals were set. We wanted to get the most out of our experience by getting deeper and deeper in the LORD. God had us helping others with information about the LORD by telling them where to start and how to start in reading the BIBLE. A lot of the information we already knew by being around my parents so we passed all of the tests. The Pastors/Teachers that were being used to teach the fundamentals used us to lead in prayer, to preach sermons and to also lead others to the LORD. College helped us mature so much that when my Dad spent time with us on break he saw the difference from when we started and now. My Dad kept staring at us in amazement of what GOD was doing in our lives.

All of us graduated from College. What is GOD going to do with us now...... Ha Ha Ha Ha Ha. Mom and Dad decided that it would be good for Bobby to stay with us at home since his Mom and Dad travel on business all the time after College. Now was the time to focus on Missionary work, and a job.

Living at home with my Mom and Dad is not really hard because they know that I follow GOD, pray, forgive, repent along with the rest of the things they taught me. We still go to church. We all still help out at the Church wherever we can. All 3 of us are taking some classes for Missionary work and looking for employment.

Bobby got a job at the hospital as a Chaplain. I think that he looks cute in his Chaplain uniform. His uniform is White and Gold. A man in a uniform. I always thought that was nice. He also preaches on Sunday with my Dad.

Jada landed a job with Missionaries Inc. where we take classes together. She gets to go on trips while taking classes. For now state to state she says. Once we graduate we will be traveling out of the country. She also preaches when needed with my Dad.

Me, I landed a job with Mom and Dad preaching at the church and Doing some Conferences from State to State.

Mom does the Bible Study, Adult Sunday School, The Ladies in White in which teaches the women young and old how to dress. The class teaches them how to carry themselves that they will be ready when their BOAZ comes. She is also over the Food/Menu for events.

Jada's Mom is in class for a Youth Minister. She is almost done. Mom and Dad allowed her to be over the Children's events and Children's Sunday School.

Ahhhhhhh look at GOD and his plan came together with friends that became family to help in the church.

TABLE OF CONTENTS

BOOK 2

CHAPTER 1: FLIGHT 128- PROPHECY BEGINS 53
CHAPTER 2: THE FLIGHT 58
CHAPTER 3: DAY 1 63
CHAPTER 4: DAY 2 67
CHAPTER 5: DAY 3 73
CHAPTER 6: DAY 4 75
CHAPTER 7: DAY 5 80
CHAPTER 8: MEETING AT THE HOUSE 82
CHAPTER 9: SHOWING HOME 84
CHAPTER 10: WEALTH OF THE LAND 87
CHAPTER 11: HISTORY OF HIM 89
CHAPTER 12: THE WEDDING 93
CHAPTER 13: A SPIRITUAL WEEK 101
CHAPTER 14: FLIGHT BACK TO THE STATES 107
CHAPTER 15: LIFE AS A HUSBAND AND WIFE 112
CHAPTER 16: LIFE WITH MY FAMILY 115

UNITED ANGEL AIRLINES
flight — 128

BOOK 2

INTRODUCTION

Every High Ranking Officer had their turn on Flight United Angel Airlines to find their Bride connected by Angels for thousands of years.

According to the history of the Ommanju family, there was a covering over them that God put on them for many generations to come because they followed God so God made a covenant with this family that the men will be great and when the time comes they will meet their bride that God allows the Angels to connect together. This connection is usually on Flight United 128.

Chapter 1

FLIGHT 128 - PROPHECY BEGINS

Mom and Dad are excited about this Conference because it is in Africa. I have never been out of the country before, so it was exciting but I was scared of the unknown. I always pray through everything asking GOD to protect me, guide me, give me wisdom in all things and sharpen the discerning of gifts to hear him audibly through stormy like situations called distractions.

I am running through the airport like a crazy woman because the Limo got to the airport late due to traffic. I didn't want to miss my flight Mom set for me or I will never hear the end of it about responsibilities.

Mom doesn't fuss loud but she is stern. So when she fusses you feel like a fire came out and burned you. HA HA HA HA HA HA HA

I keep playing it in my head over and over and she says to use your gifts to hear GOD'S instructions. This is a very important trip. This time let the angels also help you that are around you.

The storm was raging as we call it. Everything seemed to be moving fast or I was moving very slow. I get to the counter to check in my luggage and the lady tells me that my flight just left and that there was nothing she could do. This time I began to cry because of hearing my Mom in my ear. I began to yell NO NO NO NO NO NO NO.

I have to get on a flight to Africa (East). I have an important conference for people who really need me to speak a word from GOD that GOD gave me. I have to stop a minute to get my composure because the lady that was speaking to me sounded muffled all of a sudden.

I YELL STOP STOP RIGHT NOW IN THE NAME OF JESUS!!!!!!!

Everyone stopped - I said can you wait one minute. I began to pray and GOD said FLIGHT 128- I told the lady that you have to have a FLIGHT 128. Where is it? How do I get to it because it goes to Africa. She asked how I know about the FLIGHT 128- I TOLD HER GOD TOLD ME!!!!!!!!

A man in a uniform from the service came from the back to escort me to FLIGHT 128.

He told me not to check my luggage so he will take them. He called for a baggage cart to come get me. Everyone began to laugh behind the counter as though they knew a secret I didn't. Well come to find out later they all did know something that I didn't.

Men on a golf cart type of vehicle come to take me to FLIGHT 128. They also had service uniforms on. I am not sure if it was the Navy or what but, they looked like gentlemen in their uniforms. Very polite like Dad taught me.

I get to this moving walkway that reminds me of a treadmill. Two men came to escort me down while the men on the cart took my luggage another way. HEYYYYYY HEYYYYYY. MY LUGGAGE, MY LUGGAGE I YELLED. They said that they went to add it to the plane. FLIGHT 128. Everyone was stressing the fact that it was FLIGHT 128. What is so special about FLIGHT 128.

As we were on the walkway a man was running to also get on this flight. It seemed as though he was running late too. He had on a uniform as they did. They told him to go around back through the other door because he had to check in. He sighed with relief. He kept thanking them because he said that the head man will kill him. He yelled before he went the other way. GOD BLESS YOU.

While we were almost at the door to the entrance another door on the side was open. All I could see was a lot of men in uniforms. No women no where except for the Flight Attendants standing in the entrance waiting. I said excuse me I am not in the service am I on the right flight? Is this FLIGHT 128? IS THIS FLIGHT 128? There must be some kind of mistake. Can you wait one moment please? They said YES MA'AM

I began to pray- LORD IS THIS CORRECT? DID I HEAR YOU RIGHT? FLIGHT 128? THE ONLY THING HE KEPT SAYING WAS FLIGHT 128 FLIGHT 128 FLIGHT 128.

Chapter 2

THE FLIGHT

All of the men were looking to see what was going on. I feel crazy right now. I never felt like this before. I always trusted GOD in what he said to do nevertheless, this feels off. As I hesitate to get on the Airlines the stewardess says WELCOME TO UNITED ANGEL AIRLINES FLIGHT 128. We will get you to your seat now. I say ok still unsure of what is going on. I follow them slowly. I am looking around as I am walking behind them. I know GOD said to not be afraid for he is with me, I am still walking slowly while looking around.

They take me to this private room right behind the PILOTS. They give me instructions to make myself comfortable. You are in good hands. They asked me if I wanted anything to drink? I smiled and said water with lemons please. Do they have lemons on this flight I whispered to myself? Oh GOD HELP ME NOW OH LORD I KEPT WHISPERING.

I could hear them snickering. They got it right away. They asked me if I was alright and did I say something? No I am alright. I kept hearing snickering from the back. Anything else Madam? I said no thank you but, thank you. As I began to sort of relax in my leather seat drinking on my water while looking out of the window through the glass I see a BIG MAN STAND ABOUT 6'5" OR TALLER VERY STOCKY IN A UNIFORM STANDING BEHIND ME. I am so scared that I turned around slowly in my chair to make sure I saw correctly. I BEGAN TO CALL ON JESUS JESUS JESUS JESUS JESUS JESUS JESUS I YELLED. Now everyone began to laugh profusely. I fainted. I wake up in this big man's arms saying Hi my name is Allen are you alright? He was holding a damp towel to my head.

You fainted. He slid the chair back to let down this bed. It was small at the same time I seem to fit perfectly. Hello my name is he interrupted to finish my sentence saying yes Amani Williams. I asked him how he knew my name? He said that GOD spoke to his heart and told him. I immediately asked him YOU KNOW GOD? He laughed, yes I know him very well. I pray to him all the time and he answers. He told me that you will be here and that you were running late like one of my officers just be patient. So you are the one he said would kill him for being late? That was Brian Jonasa- a good kid. Yes I am the head commander here therefore you are in good hands. YES I AM I HAVE GOD I SAID! He laughed. Yes you do you are here.

The flight will take 5 days, that is why they brought your luggage with you. They stop a couple of places in between the flight to get fuel. He assured me that I was in good hands. He is smiling big. His smile is friendly and I began to not feel threatened as much. He seems to be a big teddy bear. I was thinking for 5 days with a man I don't know.

OK LORD HELP ME OUT HERE. I NEED YOUR HELP LORD. I AM CALLING ON YOU LORD TO HELP ME. OH MY LORD. THE LORD BEGAN TO LAUGH. TRUST ME HE SAID. It sounds like he was very very happy.

I got up to open the door to the back to see what they were doing despite Allen telling me I was in good hands. All I could see were angels in every row.

LORD WHAT ARE YOU UP TO? I HEAR HIM LAUGH AGAIN.

This time I could hear angels singing as he laughed. I can't wait to tell Mom I thought to myself. Allen and I began to talk a little and then more and more. If GOD says it's OK then it is ok I trust him and I believe him. For I love him and he loves me.

It was time to get fuel by that time a day had passed. Time seemed to just run past. I don't remember going to the bathroom before the flight. Now I have to use it badly. One of the flight attendants guided me to my restroom. She said it was set just for me shower and all.

She told me that I have about 3 hours before take off. It takes a lot of time to get fueled before I go to the door.

Chapter 3

DAY 1

I opened the door and LORD and behold the most beautiful room I have ever seen. Flowers galore all around as another flight attendant meets me to give me a tour. That was just the entryway. We go into another room with flowers- candy- chocolate - fruit- plenty of drinks such as juices- water with fruit in it. Soft music filled the air. There was a chase with a silk gown laid out with slippers.

A vanity with flowers on it and a card that says WELCOME-(Allen) I pray you feel at home. A brush, a comb, whatever I needed to do my hair with was there. I thought to myself AWWWWWWW how sweet.

I was escorted to a jacuzzi that was filled with bubbles and a glass of sparkling grape juice with candles all around. How romantic I thought. If he is trying to seduce me it is not going to work I said sternly. She just laughed.

I got in the jacuzzi. As I began to relax and close my eyes I feel some hands cover my eyes. For the first time in my life I CUSSED. What the HELLLLL! I opened my eyes and it was Jada. I cried and screamed OH MY GOD!!!!!!!!!! OH MY GOD !!!!!!!!!! WHAT ARE YOU DOING HERE?

Girl I thought you were some guy trying to get my goodies. We began to laugh so hard. There are no guys in sight. What are you talking about? Again how did you know I was here? GOD told me. GOD told you? YES GOD TOLD ME! YES GOD TOLD ME!!!!!! I am on flight 333 going to Africa. I am going to Africa too East Africa. I am going to West Africa on a missionary job. Oh ok, they said that they were fueling up. Us too. I have to go now we hugged. We both yelled I LOVE YOU at the same time as I watched her go through the door.

The Stewardess let me know that it was time to go back to the plane in about 15 minutes, I shook my head OK and got dressed in some jeans and a cute top left out for me. It was purple, a beautiful silk top with purple slipper shoes to match.

By the time I was escorted to my seat on the plane Allen was standing at the entrance of the door with the same colors on. He held out his arm to escort me to my seat.

I was staring at him without his uniform on. He was gorgeous. Muscles bulging out everywhere, a pretty smile, and a nice clean haircut. He smelled amazingly good. He reminded me of Sampson but I sure was not Delilah I thought to myself. I began to feel embarrassed, I asked for forgiveness because I never felt like this before.

I feel like my dream as a little girl was coming true. I think I better pinch myself to make sure. I pinched myself hard- ouch I yelled.

Allen said what are you doing? I responded trying to wake myself up from this wonderful dream. We both began to laugh. We talked all night long until I fell asleep.

Chapter 4

DAY 2

Excited to see what was next Allen tells me that we get to spend the entire day together.

When I go out, we are on a private beach with everything you could think of. Romantic clear water that you can see the little fish swim by. The sand was warm, white and flowers everywhere. Soft romantic music was playing. I was in awe of all the beauty that I didn't notice no one on the plane but me and Allen with the airline stewardess.

I also didn't notice the red carpet laid out with flowers all over it as though we were getting married. I began to laugh and think in jeans. My Mom would kill me….. Without her knowing Mom would kill me.

Are you alright Allen asked? Yes, I began to laugh at the crazy thought.

He walks me to this beautiful mansion so beautiful outside I began to just look in amazement. I pinched myself again. Do you think you are dreaming again? Yes noticing his beautiful brown eyes as he picks me up to cross the threshold. Anything for you Amani anything for you.

He takes me on a tour of the house. I say this is so beautiful Allen is all I could think of. He laughed. He has been smiling since I got back on the plane from the first surprise.

He takes me to this room with romantic gowns laid out. He tells me to pick one and meet him downstairs. I now ask the LORD what is going on here?

OK LORD WHAT COLOR SHOULD I WEAR? BLUE! OK LORD BLUE IT IS.

Slippers are there to match. I put them on. I am on my way to the stairs and he yells STOP RIGHT THERE AT THE TOP OF THE STAIRS SMILING FROM EAR TO EAR. A gentleman in a uniform comes up to escort me to Allen. I see Allen is still in his purple silk shirt and jeans. He holds out his arm to escort me. I look at him. Hey you are the soldier that was late? YUP. I would not miss this for nothing in the world while he is smiling big. That smile was not there long. A serious look came across his face as we walked down the stairs to Allen.

When I got to Allen I whispered to him. I don't feel fresh in this dress. Can I go somewhere to freshen up? He laughed so hard. When he stopped laughing he said yes my dear. He took me to another part of the house that had a big jacuzzi with bubble, candles, and flowers galore. My sparkling grape juice was on the side with chilled glasses.

ALLEN ALLEN ALLEN I am yelling trying to get his attention from the gaze in his eyes as though he was on another planet. I have to get to Africa. I have a Conference to get to. UHHHHHHHHHHHHHHH he said nonchalantly.... Enjoy my dear, just relax.

As he escorted me in the water with my gown on. I am yelling again ALLEN ALLEN ALLEN I still have my gown on. Dear just relax is all he kept saying. Trust GOD he said.

Relax I will check on you in about 15 minutes. By the time I opened my eyes he had a goldish brown gown with slippers to match on the chair by the vanity. I asked him to leave as I got dressed. He left. I took the blue gown off to hurry back to the jacuzzi to get fresh. Ahhhhhh yes now I feel better. I got dressed just as I was about to finish getting dressed. There was a knock on the door. My dear are you alright. Yes I yelled.

I tried to get to the door in a quick fashion when I saw myself in this gorgeous mirror. Wow this gown is so beautiful. WHAT IS GOING ON LORD? I HAVE NEVER FELT LIKE THIS LORD HELP ME.

Allen I really have to get to my Conference or my Mom and Dad will kill me. He ignored me by saying TRUST GOD MY DEAR. TRUST GOD.

He guided me to this big room with our dinner laid out on this beautiful table. I could not help but smile and whisper THANK YOU LORD FOR ALL THAT YOU HAVE DONE FOR ME.

When dinner was over he led me to this other room. A ballroom where we danced for hours.

Allen I am a little tired. Alright my dear. He picks me up and takes me upstairs to this big room with a huge bed with rose petals all over it. He lays me on the bed. He walks away. Goodnight my dear. He closes the door.

When I woke up, I saw something on the vanity. I had to see what was there. there was a note on the vanity - I pray you like all what GOD has planned for you. There is more to come my dear, TRUST GOD. Allen.

There were jewels of gold on the most beautiful necklace I have ever seen with matching earrings a bracelet to match. I began to cry because everything was so beautiful.

My dear are you dressed he asked from behind the closed door. Yes Allen as I stood up to show off what he had out for me. To my surprise he had the same colors on to match. He we go matching again. He laughed so hard as he began to smile so big.

He escorted me to the same big room with the big dining room table. It was dressed as though we were out for fine dining. He pulls out my chair. He put the napkin on my lap. He plays like I am so heavy that he can't skoot in my chair…. We both laugh….. Are you alright my dear. Yes Allen I am fine. He pours me some sparkling grape juice. I am looking at the glass in amazement. It was crystal. You like my dear? Yes Allen it is so beautiful is all that I kept saying. I feel like I am in a fairytale. Thank you so very much for all that you have done for me. Anything for you my dear. A waiter came out with dinner.

Chapter 5

DAY 3

I woke up to a light bell ringing. Wake up my dear I have breakfast for you. I opened my eyes and I had my golden gown still on along with all of the jewelry he gave me.

As I was eating OH MY GOD THIS WAS SO GOOD. THANK YOU LORD, I YELLED. We both laughed so hard. I realized that this is why GOD was laughing. He had many gifts for me to enjoy. THANK YOU LORD. As I began to finish up Allen had laid out me an outfit. A white top pure cotton the tag said with some blue jeans. OH MY GOD! Jewelry again. Red beautiful jewels again. Necklace, earrings, and a bracelet to match. My dear we leave in an hour please get ready. As he was leaving OK I will, I said excitedly. Thank you as he spoke through the door.

Chapter 6

DAY 4

He escorted me out to the plane. When I entered it I noticed that it was a different plane. Cream colored seats, marble tables with fresh fruit, chocolates and finger foods to snack on. A variety of fruit in the water. Rose petals everywhere.

I have a surprise for you my dear. What is it Allen? By this time I am relaxed but I have not yet put 2 and 2 together of what my parents always told me that GOD had many gifts for me. He gave me a big bag. Open it! It had lots of paper over the gift whatever it was. I snatched out all of the paper. There was a big stuffed lion under all of that paper. HAHAHAHAHAAHAHA. We laughed so hard together. We said at the same time. THE LION OF THE TRIBE OF JUDAH. We started singing the song by Deitrick Haddon - Oh Judah let me hear you say. We could not stop laughing. Ok my dear we are on our way.

We have to get fuel Allen my dear. Alright no problem. By this time I am so in LOVE with this man that I don't know what to do.

We set down to get fuel there is this beautiful Chapel further in the distance. Allen can we go to the Chapel I would like to pray? Yes my dear anything for you Amani. All I ask is that you change clothes to freshen up we have a long way to go. No more stopping.

He shows me where to go. Before you go my dear we have 2 hours before we leave. I want to make it before night fall in Africa. Yes Allen.

More surprises - A cream colored dress with blue jewels- a necklace,a bracelet, earrings, and this time a ring. I gasp for air because it is so beautiful. This time I take a shower to rush to see what Allen has on.

Same colors again. We said at the same time WE MATCH. We began to laugh. Come on my dear let's go to the Chapel.

Off to the Chapel we walk but when we get in it is decorated for a wedding as it is so beautiful. As we sat down to pray I asked GOD, LORD IS THIS HIM? GOD SAID YES! I began to cry AND PRAISE GOD…. THANK YOU JESUS THANK YOU JESUS…… I see my Mom, Dad, Bobby, Jada and Jada's Mom walk out. I began to scream with joy to see them all.

What are you doing here? I am yelling. I am so happy that I forgot where I was for a moment. OHHHHHHHH LORD PLEASE FORGIVE ME FOR DISRESPECTING YOUR HOUSE.

I whisper to Mom and Dad IT'S HIM IT'S HIM.

Amani my dear I ask you in front of your parents and friends. WILL YOU GIVE ME GREAT PLEASURE FOR THE REST OF LIFE TO BE MY WIFE BY MARRYING ME? He was on one knee as he asked.

We all started screaming again and jumping up and down with joy. I said YES ALLEN YES as we kissed everyone was clapping and screaming HALLELUJAH HALLELUJAH HALLELUJAH

WE ALL YELL THANK YOU LORD.

I told Allen that I prayed. I asked GOD were you him? GOD SAID YES! GOD told me after I prayed to let GOD know that I was ready for my wife. GOD TOLD ME YOUR NAME. I have been in love since.

Is that why we switched planes? Yes we had to go and get your parents and friends.

So Mom and Dad you knew what this trip meant? YES GOD TOLD US WHEN YOU WERE BORN. ALL WE COULD SAY WAS GOD HAD GOOD PLANS FOR YOU.

THANK YOU JESUS!!!!!!! On our way to Africa.

After we get on the jet Allen turns to me Amani here you go. Here are the keys to our house and our Jet. OHHHHHH WOW NO WAY. That was one of them. He put the keys on a fuzzy ball that was pink. I gave him the biggest kiss.

Chapter 7

DAY 5

We make it to Africa. As I was looking out of the window I noticed how beautiful, green and the water looks so good. We landed at this airport. There is a limousine waiting for Mom, Dad Jada, Bobby and Jada's Mom. Beautiful is all that I can say. Beautiful has been my favorite word the whole trip to describe things. Allen made sure everyone was in. He told the driver to take them to the house. I yelled to everyone I LOVE YOU AND SEE YOU SOON.

Here comes our limousine with honorable escorts top of the line Hummer, Lights flashing while the sirens are going. I felt so special. GOD TOLD ME ALL MY LIFE HE HAS GOOD PLANS FOR ME THROUGH MY PARENTS. NOW I SEE THAT HE DID. FOR THAT I AM GRATEFUL. Tears began to flow from my eyes for the joy of the LORD is great.

Chapter 8

MEETING AT THE HOUSE

Allen and myself finally make it to this huge house out runs this lady and this man to meet the car. Amani my dear these are my parents Meagan Ommanju and Edward Ommanju who is a Retired Commander.

His Mom is just hugging and kissing me. Happy to see Me. They are yelling let me see you my girl, let me see you.

They are so happy that we go inside and there is more family along with my Mom and Dad along with friends I call family.

There is James Ommanju Allen's brother - Commanding Officer

Amanda Ommanju- His sister

Daniel Ommanju - His little brother

They said God told us you were coming we had to prepare quickly. God told us what to get.

Chapter 9

SHOWING HOME

While Allen was showing me around with me on his arm his parents were showing Mom and Dad around. James was showing Jada around. Daniel and Amanda were showing Bobby around.

To our surprise - God told Bobby about Amanda - God told James about Jada. God revealed the details to the parents but not the kids. All they have to say is Lord I am ready for a wife then God gives them a Wife.

I am sad for Bobby's Parents because they could not make it. Bobby said that they were away on Business. To our surprise the doorbell rings and it's Bobby's Parents.

Cindy and Richard Branch

Now this is beautiful.

According to the things that we have seen, the Ommanju family was very wealthy in Africa. As Bobby and Amanda were spending time together Bobby asks Amanda to marry him. Daniel still has a ways to go before he is ready for his wife.

James Allen's brother spoiled Jada as much as Allen spoiled me. He asked Jada to marry him too.

The Ommanju family had something planned special for Amanda and Bobby. Amanda Parents gave them $10 Million Dollars in which was for their wedding present when they are ready. I am not sure of how much that is in currency here in Africa or what it is called here.God had a good plan for us all. Everyone was happy.

Chapter 10

WEALTH OF THE LAND

3 Limos pulled up in the front for us to see what Allen's parents wanted to show everyone.

About 5 miles away Allen's Dad invested in a little city called the Ommanju Divisions. It had stores that were Modern, but not expensive. They had nice Hotels, dined with City Lights. They wanted visitors to see the progress of Africa.

We are still in the cars viewing the sights about 30 minutes out of the city we come to a town or village. The people are yelling thank you God for Ommanju. Thank you God for Ommanju. Allen's Mom and Dad were helping to build houses for people to live well. They had a Market for the people to get food and clothing. He gave the people each money to start a new life.

Allen's Parents tell us to get out to view the city as they explain everything their eyes lit up. They thanked God for allowing them to help others.

Allen's Parents also own a construction company to help the people have jobs for the Men to take care of their families. It was called Ommanju Family Construction.

Allen's Parents said that when you give God gives back. They said that when your hand is closed God cannot put anything in it. We all agreed and said AMEN.

Allen's Parents introduced all of the people to us so that they can also get to know us.

Chapter 11

HISTORY OF HIM

When we all returned to the house it was ready for supper in the Lavish Dining Room. The table was set, but no food was out just yet. They were waiting for us to sit at the table. Allen's Dad requested that we freshen up for supper and then meet back in the dining room.

Allen's Mom asked for the women to come with her and Allen's dad asked for the men to follow him.

While we were with his Mom she was giving us gowns and jewelry to wear for the dinner before freshening up. She said that the jewelry was passed down generations and that they were special to her.

When we were done the men were standing by the door in Tuxedos in a line waiting to escort us to our seats. Tonight Allen's Dad had wine for everyone to drink except Daniel because he was too young right now. He said that he was saving it for a special time such as this.

When dinner was over Allen's Mom and Dad asked for everyone to meet in the family room to explain the History of the Ommanju Family.

The History Of The Ommanju Family:

According to Allen's father Edward Ommanju history started with his great great grandfather Baldwin Ommanju. Baldwin Ommanju gave his life to God when a tragic event happened to him while in the service. His wife prayed constantly because she said that that was all she knew to do. Baldwin didn't know God until the night before he passed away. It was said that Baldwin's wife helped him with the help from God to give his life to Christ. Edward's Father was named Eric Ommanju a Commanding Officer in the Service who met his wife on Flight 128. It was told by Allen's Father that the soldiers that were on the plane were all of the soldiers that passed away while in the service.

It was told that on the day Baldwin Ommanju gave his life to God, God promised him that there will be a covering over his family for many generations to come. He told him that it was a Covenant between him and God. God gave him instructions to follow when time to meet the woman he chose for him. He told him that for constant prayers with the pure heart that every man in the Ommanju family will have wealth to take good care of the women in the family. God told him that all of the men are to learn as he did and the women are to learn how to become prepared to become Queens for their mate for generations to come.

The story was amazing how God can use people to help people I thought. It made me fall deeper in love with Allen and his family for having such honorable men to follow God's instructions and plan.

Thank you Jesus we all said after the story and began to laugh at the same time. It shows that the family is becoming one and one accord.

Look how God uses a family to change people, help people, and use them for his Glory. That's the kind of God I serve I thought while smiling.

Chapter 12

THE WEDDING

What we didn't know is that Allen's Mom and Dad have a massive church built so that others can know about God. He wanted them to love God as he did. He also wanted for them to worship freely without feeling as though it was wrong to worship God. After all he said God has blessed his family for many generations so why not bless God with " A Temple Of Prayer" it was called. The construction workers have been working on it day and night. What we didn't know is that it was ready for me and Allen's wedding. Then James and Jada- then Bobby and Amanda. We found out the plan about the wedding. Amanda knew nothing of the Temple because it was a big surprise.

"Time For The Wedding"- Preparation

Allen's Mom tells us that it is time after breakfast as she is all of a sudden excited after speaking with Allen's Dad due to God telling him while they were in prayer that it was time.

Allen's Mom told all of the women to come with her and Allen's Dad told the men to come with him. Allens Father said that we only have 5 days to do everything.

Everyone was excited because they did not know what to expect.

The Date will be August 8th - 8 for new beginnings and 8 for new beginnings

New beginnings is the meaning of the number 8 according to God's Numbers - the number 5 means Grace from God.

What we also did not know that all three weddings were on the same exact day.

The Plan God set was to be:

Bobby and Amanda first-James and Jada second-Then Allen and myself last. God said that he had separate plans for us all Allen's Dad said. I am so happy that God's plans are so good.

Allen's Mom flew us (the women) to a lady she knows named Banta Maraha. Her family has been making dresses for generations- she was never married but hoped God had someone special for her. She said she never lost faith. She said she just keeps thanking God every day while smiling. She was about Daniel's age owning her own company making dresses.

She told us that for generations God told her family what kind of dress to make and the color of the material to use. As we were approaching this room there were 3 garment bags ready with only our First Name on it. Our mouths dropped in amazement. We were about to ask how she knew, but she stopped us by saying God told her. We all laughed. What we didn't know is that her family has made dresses for all of the Ommanju women for generations including Allen's Mom. We also didn't know that Allen's Mom and Dad has taken care of her family for years. She says that they are good people and that God has his hand on this family. She stressed how she loved them. She said that Allen's Mom and Dad were like her Mom and Dad. She said that while her parents were traveling Allen's Mom and Dad took great care of her and that they gave her family a house while making dresses. In the house behind one of their other homes. I guess you could say the Guest House. That is what we called it in the states. Now we had to go. She locked up everything and grabbed her bags to leave with us. She is to get us ready for the Weddings. So Many surprises.

We get back to the house to take the dresses to Allen's Mom's room so that no one peeks. Awwwwww all of us said and then laughed, me, Jada, and Amanda. Now I have more sisters that I love so much- Amanda said we all hugged. Allen's Mom just stood there with Banta, My Mom, Jada's Mom smiling big while thanking God for this blessed moment. Amanda considered Banta to be her sister since they were so close to her family.

It was coming upon the 5th Day in which was the 8-8 tomorrow. Banta, Me, Amanda and Jada stayed up all night because we couldn't sleep while being filled with excitement. The men were not allowed to see us until the time of the Wedding.

Allen's Mom explained to us. All of the Moms came in to sit with us.

Allen's Mom was giving gifts to all of us including Banta because she was a daughter to her too. The jewelry she gave us was amazing. She gave me a bunch of Pearls, Jada some Emeralds, Banta some Blue Sapphire and Amanda the most beautiful jewels Chocolate Diamonds. All of the jewelry was our favorite that we all said at the same time as we looked at the jewelry she gave us.

God Knows all - laughing together

Allen's Mom explains how we are to get Amanda together first and that we are to pick the color of RED with GOLD on it for her Wedding. BLUE WITH GOLD for Jada's Wedding. WHITE WITH GOLD for Amani's Wedding. All of our favorite colors.

She explains how it is very important that we spend the rest of time with our husbands after the wedding before leaving for the states. We were to spend a week in the Private part of the house set for all of the brides and grooms in separate quarters to connect with God as a couple. Time to go to bed - The girls stay together and the Moms went to their room. Being exhausted we all finally go to sleep.

Allen's Mom is waking us up by saying PRAISE GOD WHAT A GLORIOUS DAY time for breakfast- Breakfast was brought in to us. It seems like breakfast since Allen made me breakfast before. She explains that we can't take too long. We have to take showers to get ready for the Weddings. Amanda is so nervous that she can't eat. Her Mom took her to the bathroom to pray with her and when she came out she was fine. Thanks Mom she said.

We finally make it to the church- Allen's Mom is giving directions to the people there to get us ready (the girls) - as we pull out the dress for Amanda- We all gasp because the dress is so beautiful. We opened the bag for Jada to see her dress and we all gasp again, her dress was so beautiful.

We opened the bag for mine and we all gasped one more time and then tears of joy ran down all of our faces. We all began to hug each other praying blessings over all couples and marriages.

Now time to get Amanda ready. As the Mothers and Banta prepare our areas with all needed for the dressing of us all. They go down the checklist to make sure nothing was left out. While we each had helpers with everything else.

Wedding Checklist:

    Gown
    Bridal Shoes
    Bridal Slip
    Lingerie
    Slip
    Garter
    Hosiery
    Jewelry
    Bridal Headpiece/Veil
    Bridal Gloves
    Bridal bouquet

Chapter 13

A SPIRITUAL WEEK

GENESIS 2:24

Therefore shall a man leave his father and his mother, and shall cleave unto his wife: and they shall become one flesh.

    Time for a Spiritual Union with our husbands. We are to pray together in the Morning at 5am after showering and wearing 100% cotton white long sheathing laying prostrate and holding hands before God. Soft music playing as we end up falling asleep while praying.

It is noon for us now. We wake up to find out that we slept after praying. We laughed together when we looked at his watch. We take another shower but this time together as husband and wife. Allen washed my hair and then conditioned it for me. He was gentle and kind. He took his time to wash me with this body wash that smells like peppermint. He asked for me to step out as he grabbed the towel to dry me off. He took the towel and patted me dry and then asked me to lay across the bed to give me a massage from all of the excitement. He said that the oil was Frankincense and Myrrh. He rubbed oil on my entire body and still a perfect gentleman. After he was done he pulled the covers down for me to get in. While he took his shower. By the time he was done I dozed off. I woke up to kisses on my face. He said that he was watching me sleep. He said that I was so beautiful and seemed to be at Peace as I slept. I didn't even notice that I hadn't eaten yet. I am so in love with the man God sent me that I can't stop smiling. To myself I continue to thank God and give him Praises for making me the happiest woman on the planet I felt. Allen had fruit and cheese with crackers for me to snack on while he picked out something for me to wear to lounge around in.

We prayed again this time we kneeled on the bed side together thanking God for the blessing of this union. As we began to say our prayer to God the words were similar we were saying. Were we becoming one? God was blending us as one to feel each other, to love each other, to think as one without speaking sort of like knowing what Allen was thinking without a word coming out of my mouth or his. Allen picked me up to put me on the bed. He went to get the lotion to put some on my feet before putting on my sandals. I was thinking it was time for us to become one intimately when he said later my love. I just wanted to enjoy the love God gave me. I began to smile again. We went to sit on the deck to notice the view as a married couple. He is holding my hand soft but firm to let me know he is there always. We began to pray again asking God to bless us when it is time for our intimate union.

We came in from the deck to see a red envelope on the floor. Another card slipped under the door to let us know that dinner was ready and at the door. We talked so much enjoying each other's company we didn't notice dinner was brought to us and waiting at the door. No one was to knock or come in while we were in our Blessing Time. Laughing together we opened the door- flowers, gifts and dinner was at the door. Allen lit the candles after setting the table with our dinners. He put our flowers in the middle. We ate to soft romantic music. He picked up his chair and sat next to mine. He began to feed me, asking for me to take small bites. We began to laugh again as he is playing like it is an airplane. After dinner we took another shower, this time he wanted me to wash him after he washed me. I didn't realize that he was very proportioned. I was in total shock when he turned around because I washed his back first. I started with his chest and went down more and more and wow my mouth dropped because he was very endowed. He began to laugh and he said it was all for me. After he rinsed he picked me up again and walked toward the bed. We woke up to the birds chirping at the window. The most beautiful birds I have seen. Two big ones and a baby sat on the ledge. It sounded like they were singing. After about 5 minutes they flew off.

We headed toward the bathroom to get started before prayer. We feel asleep again holding hands while praying. This time while getting up I was a little dizzy. As usual Allen picked me up and headed toward the bed to lie down and then run to get me a cool towel to put across my forehead. He called his mother on the emergency phone in the hallway. He was excited in urgency to get me help. His mother told him to calm down God planted a seed in me. Allen began to laugh and thank God.

He came running in to tell me the news. I began to thank God and pray for a healthy baby. It was another blessing to look forward to. He said his mother said to keep it hush hush till time. Allen explained to me. Allen began kissing me so lovingly and then kissing my stomach. As he put me on the bed to sit he put his hand on my stomach and began to pray to God for a name. God told him Abraham. Allen began to shout with joy. We began to become intimate again. I felt as though I never wanted to leave this room so much love filled the room. We continued our journey of praying and intimacy the week flew by. The last day of waking up the room was filled with angels confirming the news of the babies name to be Abraham. They also had the news that there was another seed planted and it was a girl. Her name was Angel. Allen was so happy he began to cry and thank God over and over again for the blessing he had given to us.

Chapter 14

FLIGHT BACK TO THE STATES

As Allen and then myself come out of the room to meet the family downstairs every couple is smiling big and giggling like teenagers with a good secret. Allen's Mother and Father already knew. This was a pretty important secret to keep until time. I couldn't even tell Mom until me and Allen agreed after the tests were confirmed to read true. We continued to hug and speak blessings to my new sisters on their marriages. Allens Mom broke up all of the hugging to give all of us a hug herself being filled with joy for us all. My Mom couldn't stop holding my hand and hugging me all the way to the table, reminding me of the Prophecy God told me about the plans he had for me. Dad hugged Allen pretty tight and continued to tell him welcome to the family my son welcome. Allen's Dad is dancing, shouting and jumping with joy all around the house praising God saying:

Thank you Father - Thank you Father - Thank you Father- Thank you Father

When he calmed down he began to weep profusely with joy thanking God. Allen took him to the Den to hug his Dad and pray with him. When God is pleased the Son always shines, he said.

Time to pack and head back to the states. As I began to pack Allen asked for me to leave everything for my Mom and Dad to take or leave with his Mom and dad to have memories of when we return. The only thing he wanted for me to take is our Wedding Attire to cherish for many many years. He said that he wanted to take me shopping to start off new together. Cars are here to take us to the Airport. We hug everyone and then get into our car. When me and Allen get to the airport it is about an hour wait. To my surprise my sisters walk up, we began to scream and jump for joy because we are on the same private jet. The men hugged and laughed at the surprise because they knew all the time. What a surprise it was. On our way all excited to see what next. Hours on the plane we are landing to find that we are in Hawaii. As the door of the plane opened we were welcomed by lots of people happy for us to be there. They welcomed us with smiles, lays and a dance. I am so into the excitement of everything I forgot we left everything behind. As we got to the hotel to check in I reminded Allen of my findings and he just laughed. If I don't know anything, I know that he had that covered. He told me that God always knows what we need.

We get to our door to the room and Allen opens the door and swoops me off of my feet to cross the threshold. Welcome my love he said. Everything I needed was there. I began to smile and thank God for a wonderful man. Allen began to spin me around and hold me as to do a little dancing saying that he is the happiest man on earth. After our showers we put on some comfortable clothes and watched a movie. The movie was Forrest Gump. Allen said he loved that movie because Forrest was so funny by being honest. We laughed and dozed off till morning ooooooohhhhhhh we must have been really tired. We woke up to a knock on the door. Allen went to the door and it was my sisters and brothers.

    James - Jada
    Bobby - Amanda
    Allen - Me Amani

Together again as a family we spend a week there in Hawaii. Off to the Capital of Washington DC for Allen and James to check- in. Oh wow I just realized that I am the wife of an Officer, a Commanding Officer. Oh Lord, I really didn't realize that when he goes off I am going to miss him. Well God will keep him well and will protect him. I have to just keep thanking God in Praise I thought to myself. Allen began to see the change of concern on my face and asked to speak with me. We went to the bathroom and he kissed me and held me tight. He said my love, everything is going to be fine. We have God with us. He took my hand to pray with him. I felt better because God filled me with peace and joy. Thank you Lord for this man. This Godly man. We came out happy.

We all spent the entire week together canoeing, fishing, romantic dinners, laughing, dancing, romantic walks and again Forrest Gump but together. Time to pack and go. Time to head toward Washington D.C.

Chapter 15

LIFE AS A HUSBAND AND WIFE

After Allen and James were done checking in they came back smiling big because they had a big check from work they forgot about. It was a bonus Allen whispered to me. We are all loaded back in the plane, I ask Allen where to next he said you know. I said yet it's a surprise. We all laughed.

Allen told me that this is the last trip together until we get the house together the way we wanted. That we need to get settled. I agreed with excitement and ready to see everything with the husband God gave me.

We land in Orlando Florida. To my surprise the limo that picked us up at the airport took us to TBN's Holyland. We did not know that Allen and James made plans while checking in to get special tickets to get in without the wait. I began to scream - ohhhhhh my God ohhhhhh my God ohhhhhhh my God. I felt like a little kid at Disneyland or Disney World because Allen was listening to my every desire. I was just thinking about the beach, sand, maybe some Beach Volleyball but never HolyLand. Oh my God I couldn't stop praising God because this is a great new beginning for us all. Allen and James pull out this pamphlet from their pockets, hand Bobby his.

While we were on a shopping spree at the Jerusalem Street Market they were planning the day. They were laughing while watching us shop and give some things to others who had a thought to buy something but didn't have the money to buy anything. The guys were very amused. We only have 8 hours to get this all in I thought to myself.

> THE GREAT TEMPLE
> CALVARY'S GARDEN TOMB
> CHURCH OF ALL NATIONS
> LIVE SHOWS AND MUCH MORE

We stayed for 4 days to get everything in to see or explore. We took a thousand pictures together and then rested. As we relax in our hotel to rest on the 4th day Allen explained to me that it is time to figure out together where we would live and what we expect from each other in a marriage. He also wanted to see if we have an idea of how many kids we wanted now that our family is beginning. Lets pray God will tell us what to do. We begin to laugh.

Chapter 16

LIFE WITH MY FAMILY

We prayed God told us what to do along with where to live. Now with our new family to come, I am grateful for making choices to pray and follow God. God knows all.

PROVERBS 15:3

THE EYES OF THE LORD ARE IN EVERY PLACE, BEHOLDING THE EVIL AND THE GOOD.

HEBREWS 13:4

MARRIAGE IS HONORABLE AMONG ALL, AND THE BED UNDEFILED; BUT FORNICATORS AND ADULTERERS GOD WILL JUDGE.

A SPECIAL THANKS TO GOD FOR ALL OF MY CHILDREN

I WOULD LOVE TO GIVE ALL PRAISES TO GOD FOR MY CHILDREN DUE TO THE PAIN IN MY HEART OF LOSING 2 CHILDREN BEFORE THE OTHER LOVES OF MY LIFE WERE BORN. I HAD A TERRIBLE HOLE IN MY HEART FOR THE LOSS OF A WOMAN NAMED INEZ AND MY 2 CHILDREN FOR QUITE SOME TIME. I THINK THAT THEY WERE THE LOVES OF MY LIFE UNTIL GOD GAVE ME MORE CHILDREN. WHEN I FOUND OUT I WAS PREGNANT I SANG TO THEM ALL THE SAME SONG. I RUBBED MY STOMACH ALL THE TIME. I WOULD PLAY GOSPEL MUSIC TO MY STOMACH FOR THEM TO HEAR. I ATE HEALTHY. I READ THE BIBLE ALL OF THE TIME TO THEM AND PLAYED SERMONS OF PREACHING TO THEM THROUGH HEADPHONES. I LOVED THEM THE BEST I KNEW HOW TO LOVE AT THAT TIME DUE TO THE HURT AND PAIN THAT I DID NOT GET OVER UNTIL I CAME TO THE UNDERSTANDING OF THE LOVE OF THE HOLY TRINITY AND IN THE EVENTS OF CHRIST JESUS ON THE CROSS. I CARRIED THE BURDEN OF GUILT OF UNFORGIVENESS ON MYSELF AND OTHERS ALONG

WITH THE QUESTIONS OF WHY THIS HAPPENED TO ME? WHY DID YOU TAKE THEM FROM ME LORD? WHAT DID I DO SO BAD TO MAKE YOU TAKE THEM FROM ME WAS SOME OF THE QUESTIONS THAT I HAD FOR GOD. WHEN GOD GAVE ME MY NEXT CHILD I WAS SO AFRAID OF A LOT OF THINGS SUCH AS IS SHE GOING TO BE ALRIGHT. WHEN THEY ALL WERE BORN I COUNTED ALL OF THEIR FINGERS AND TOES BECAUSE OF THE DEFORMATION OF THEIR OLDER BROTHER. I ALSO WANTED TO HOLD THEM SO THAT THEY WOULD KNOW THAT I LOVED THEM AND FEEL IT WHEN I HELD THEM BEFORE THE NURSE TOOK THEM TO BE CLEANED.

GOD I THANK YOU FOR MY HUSBAND

I WOULD LOVE TO GIVE THANKS TO GOD FOR MY HUSBAND BISHOP LAMONT JONES FOR BEING THERE WHEN THE CREATIVITY OF THIS BOOK WAS GIVEN TO ME BY GOD. GOD ALLOWED FOR HIM TO GIVE ME THE PEACE AND QUIET THAT ALL WRITERS NEED TO CREATE SOMETHING GREAT. WE TOGETHER WENT THROUGH THE STRUGGLES OF THE BAD ALONG WITH THE HAPPINESS OF THE GOOD AND THE GRADUAL EVOLUTION OF GROWTH. GOD SAID IN HIS WORD THAT IRON SHARPENS IRON IN WHICH IS SO TRUE IN OUR CASE.

I GIVE PRAISE TO GOD FOR MY FRIENDS

I WOULD LOVE TO GIVE PRAISES TO GOD FOR MY FRIENDS WHO CRIED FOR ME BECAUSE THEY KNEW THE TRIALS AND TRIBULATIONS I WAS GOING THROUGH BUT THEY KNEW I HAD JESUS. THE ONES WHO WERE HAPPY FOR ME BECAUSE I WAS DOING SOMETHING I SET OUT TO DO. FOR THE FRIENDS THAT GOD DELETED BECAUSE THEY WERE NOT ABLE TO GO ON THIS JOURNEY WITH ME. FOR ALL OF THE NEW FRIENDS GOD GAVE ME THAT JUST LOVE ME FOR ME.

I WOULD LOVE TO GIVE HONOR TO GOD FOR MY SISTER

I would love to give honor to God for my little **SISTER (KLJ)** my **TWIN** as we call each other. Every since we met all those years ago we just clicked. We always had our differences in opinions in which turned out perfect. I was always trying to show you the good in the world that was so bad growing up. I finally cleaned my glasses and saw the world you were speaking to me about. It was terrible. I began to feel numb with the hurt and pain we endured together and separately in our lives. We were both screaming but no one heard us. We lost contact for a while and then came back together. God always has us on a road that merges back together. What I love about you is that you are always where I can find you……. You are always the one to stay put while I was the one to always use my wings to fly… So this is for you my sister whom I love dearly. Our journey is one that will NEVER END when God has the last say. COME TASTE AND SEE THAT THE LORD IS GOOD. TEARS OF A CLOWN IS JUST A SONG.

LETTER OF APPRECIATION TO THE PEOPLE IN THE CITIES THAT I HAVE JOURNEYED TO

I WOULD LOVE TO THANK ALL OF THE PEOPLE THAT HAVE LOVED ME WITH THEIR TRUE HEARTS FOR WHO I AM. I ALSO WANT TO THANK ALL OF THE PEOPLE THAT I HAVE MET THAT HAVE BEEN A BLESSING TO ME BY SHOWING ME THE GRATITUDE OF THEIR HEARTS TO HELP ME WHILE ON MY JOURNEY. MY JOURNEY HAVE NOT BEEN EASY FOR ME ESPECIALLY THROUGH THE TRANSITION OF GROWTH, MATURITY, HURT AND PAIN I WAS EXPERIENCING. MAY GOD BLESS YOU AND AND YOUR FAMILIES. AMEN

"What A Friend Means To Me"

A Friend Is A 🎁 From The Lord.
A Friend Is Like Pennies From Heaven wanting To Send Time With You when Sad And Discouraged Or Unfriendly.

A Friend Is Like An Open 📖 Wanted To Be Known And To Have Around To Enjoy.

A Friend Is A Ray Of ☀️ Shine Ready To Brighten Your Day.
A Friend Is A Blanket Wrapped In Love.

A Friend's ✋ And ❤️ is present When Needed.
Honestly Is Equal To Friendship.!"
To Say And Know You Will Be There is A Friend Indeed!!!
Friends Are Like Flowers That Grows.!"
Friends Make Things Beautiful !!!
"If You Want Friend You Have To Be One!!!"
"A Friend Is Two Peas In A Pot!
"Freinds Are Like Angels Unexpected!!!"
"Friend Is A pleasure To Have Just Like You" !!!

"That's What Friends Are For"!!!!

"From My Heart To Yours!"

From Kisha 2020